Novena Prayers & Devotions

Brother Daniel Korn, C.Ss.R.

Liguori

ONE LIGUORI DRIVE
LIGUORI MO 63057-9999

Imprimi Potest:
Richard Thibodeau, C.Ss.R.
Provincial, Denver Province
The Redemptorists

Imprimatur:
Most Reverend Michael J. Sheridan
Auxiliary Bishop, Archdiocese of St. Louis

ISBN 0-7648-0760-9
Library of Congress Catalog Card Number: 2001091027

Except where noted, Scripture quotations are from the *New
Revised Standard Version of the Bible*, copyright © 1989 by
the Division of Christian Education of the National Council
of Churches of Christ in the USA. Used with permission. All
rights reserved.

All other Scripture quotations are from the *Christian Community Bible*, Catholic Pastoral Edition, © 1995, Liguori
Publications. All rights reserved.

The Novena of Confidence in the Sacred Heart of Jesus
(adapted) is reprinted by permission of the Society of the
Sacred Heart.

Quotation on page 6 of Saint Thérèse of Lisieux is from *The Final
Conversations*, tr. John Clarke (Washington: ICS, 1977), 102.

To order, call 1-800-325-9521
www.liguori.org
www.catholicbooksonline.com

Contents

Novena Prayers

Litanies

Novena of Confidence in the Immaculate Heart of Mary

What Is a Novena?

Devotion to the Holy Trinity and prayers and novenas in honor of the Blessed Virgin Mary and the saints are moments of shared friendship with the court of heaven. Through our friendship with the community of saints, we are assisted in our daily striving to live our lives steeped in deep love of God and neighbor. Like the holy ones who have gone before us, we strive to be a light in the world, bringing the compassion and love of God to all we meet in our journey of life.

In its great document on the Church, *Lumen gentium*, Vatican II has this to say about how the saints help us:

Being more closely united to Christ, those who dwell in heaven fix the whole

Church more firmly in holiness.…They do not cease to intercede with the Father for us, as they proffer the merits which they acquired on earth through the one mediator between God and [human beings], Christ Jesus.…So by their… concern is our weakness greatly helped. (49)

The *Catechism of the Catholic Church* (956) clearly shows us this concern of the saints when it gives us the dying words of Saint Dominic:

Do not weep, for I shall be more useful to you after my death, and I shall help you then more effectively than during my life.

and those of Saint Thérèse of Lisieux:

I want to spend my heaven in doing good on earth.

Novenas to our Lord and in honor of Mary and the saints are good ways to relate to them in the midst of our daily lives. Through these prayers and devotions, we bring them into our lives and share with them our needs and worries. We ask Mary and the saints to join their prayers with ours, and as we do, our friendships with them grow.

One day when I was busy cleaning the church, I saw a woman standing in front of the statue of Saint Anne. As I passed by, I heard her saying, "Thank you, Saint Anne, for helping me." That simple act of familiarity with a saint inspired me. Saint Anne was really a friend to that woman.

Saint Alphonsus Liguori, founder of the Redemptorist Congregation, wrote many books on spirituality. Whenever I read them, I always feel as though I have just been included in a conversation among saints, as though I am in a room with Saints Bernard, Teresa of Ávila, John of the Cross, Bridget, and many others, all sitting in a circle conversing with

Alphonsus. I am left with a feeling of familiarity with these holy men and women.

In these examples, we experience what the Church tells us about our relationship with the court of heaven. The saints are our helpers and friends and stand ready to lead us to a deeper experience of God.

In this collection of novenas and prayers, we have presented those that are most popular, as well as prayers in honor of some recently beatified and canonized saints. Here you will also find a section on how to make a novena to your patron saint or any heavenly friend of your choice. While the traditional novena is a prayer or prayers repeated on nine consecutive days, these novenas and prayers may be used in a number of ways to enhance your prayer life. May our Lord and his Blessed Mother, along with the angels and saints, surround you with all that is good and holy.

Blessed be God in the angels and in the saints!

Novenas

To the Most Holy Trinity

In the name of the Father, and of the Son, and of the Holy Spirit. Amen

Blessed be the Most Holy Trinity, both now and forever. Amen

SCRIPTURE READING
MATTHEW 28:19-20, CCB

Go, therefore, and make disciples from all nations. Baptize them in the Name of the Father and of the Son and of the Holy Spirit, and teach them to fulfill all that I have commanded you. I am with you always until the end of this world.

SILENT REFLECTION

REFLECTION PRAYER

Most Holy Trinity, Father, Son and Holy Spirit,
I come before you in prayerful adoration. Surround me with the radiance of your healing
light. God from God, Light from Light, true
God from true God! Blessed are you in the
glory of your majesty! I believe in you, I hope
in you, I love you. Blessed Trinity, one God,
have mercy on me.

I adore you, Holy and Eternal One, Creator of
all that is and will be. You are the fount of
everlasting mercy. In you the whole universe
lives and has its origin. You surround me with
a Father's love and hold us to yourself as a
Mother holding her infant close to her breast.
Cover me with your mercy and compassion.
Open my mind and soul to the presence of
your being, and lead me in the path of peace
and love.

Holy God, Holy Mighty One, Holy Immortal One, have mercy on me.

I adore you, Jesus Christ, Son of the Living God. While all was in quiet silence and the night was in the middle of its course, you, the Word of the Father, leapt down from heaven into our world as loving Redeemer and Healer. You have revealed the face of the Father. In you and through your passion, death, and resurrection, we were consecrated and made into a new creation. Grant that I may follow in the footsteps of your gospel teachings and bring to the world your mercy and forgiveness by my deeds of loving concern for others.

Holy God, Holy Mighty One, Holy Immortal One, have mercy on me.

I adore you, Holy Spirit, Lord and giver of life, who proceed from the Father and the Son. You are the guest of my soul, the teacher and consoler of my life. I ask you to open my mind and heart to your anointing and power. In times

of difficulty, inspire me to choose what is right.
When I am afraid, surround me with your light,
and give me courage to profess my faith.
Gentle Spirit of Jesus, come to me and lead
me in the way of truth and peace.

*Holy God, Holy Mighty One, Holy Immortal
One, have mercy on me.*

Most Holy Trinity, Father, Son, and Holy
Spirit, I adore you and offer you my praise
and thanksgiving for all the blessings you have
showered upon me. You have created me in
your own image and likeness. Grant that all
my thoughts, words, and actions be according
to your holy will. May my life be a praise of
glory to you, Most Holy Trinity. Glory and
praise to you forever and ever. Amen

Maker, Lover, and Keeper,
Father, Son, and Holy Spirit,
Surrounding us in holy light,
Ever Blessed Trinity.

To the Holy Spirit

Come, Holy Spirit. Fill the hearts of your faithful, and make the fire of your love burn within them. Send forth your Spirit, and there shall be a new creation. And you shall renew the face of the earth.

SCRIPTURE READING
1 CORINTHIANS 12:7-11, CCB

The Spirit reveals his presence in each one with a gift which is also a service. One is to speak with wisdom, through the Spirit. Another teaches according to the same Spirit. To another is given faith, in which the Spirit acts; to another the gift of healing, and it is the same Spirit. Another works miracles, another is a prophet, another recognizes what comes from the good or evil spirit; another speaks in tongues, and still another interprets what has been said in tongues.

And all of this is the work of the one and only Spirit, who gives to each one as he so desires.

Prayer to the Holy Spirit
by Saint Alphonsus Liguori

Most Holy Spirit, the Paraclete, I offer you this most cold heart of mine. I pray you to pierce it with a ray of your light and a spark of your fire. Melt the hardness and coldness that sometimes enters my heart.

You are the Divine Spirit. Give me courage against all evil I may encounter this day.

You are the Fire. Enkindle in me your love.

You are the Light. Enlighten my mind with knowledge.

You are the Dove. Give me innocence and simplicity of heart.

You are the gentle Breeze. Calm the storms in my life.

You are the Tongue of Fire. Teach me how to praise you in all things.

You are the Cloud. Shelter me in the shadow of your protection.

Holy Spirit, you are the guest of my soul, the promised gift of Jesus sent to be with us always. Hear my prayer and help me in my most urgent need. *(Here mention your requests.)* Glory and praise to the Most Holy Trinity, now and always. Amen

Spirit of Jesus Prayer

Spirit of Jesus, come to me. Enable me to think like Jesus Christ, to will like Jesus Christ, to act and suffer like Jesus Christ. Holy Spirit, fill me with a lively interest in my divine Savior, with the desire to please him, the longing to imitate him, the need to resemble him. Grant that Jesus may live in me through Mary. Amen

To the
Sacred Heart of Jesus

Feast Day: Friday following the Second Sunday after Pentecost

Come to me, all you that are weary and are carrying heavy burdens, and I will give you rest. Take my yoke upon you, and learn from me; for I am gentle and humble in heart, and you will find rest for your souls. For my yoke is easy, and my burden is light.

Matthew 11:28-30

Merciful Heart of Jesus, you are the abode of loving forgiveness. In the symbol of your Sacred Heart, I see an image of tenderness and compassion. I offer you my poor and needy heart. Accept this simple gift of myself and unite me to your Sacred Heart. In your Heart, I find comfort, peace, and a safe harbor of protection. In your Heart are justice and love, wisdom and knowledge.

Loving Heart of my Redeemer, help me in my time of need. *(Here state your intentions.)* Jesus my Savior, the Father is well pleased with you and has glorified you in your holy passion and Resurrection. Draw me close to your compassionate heart.

Sacred Heart of Jesus, I offer you my thoughts, words, and actions. Take them and use them for your glory and honor. Through devotion to your Sacred Heart, may I become an instrument of peace and reconciliation. Amen

Sacred Heart of Jesus, have mercy on me!

SCRIPTURE READING
JOHN 19:34-37

One of the soldiers pierced his side with a spear, and at once blood and water came out. (He who saw this has testified so that you also may believe. His testimony is true, and he knows that he tells the truth.) These things occurred so that the scripture might be fulfilled, "None of his bones shall be broken." And again another passage of scripture says, "They will look on the one whom they have pierced."

SILENT REFLECTION

REFLECTION PRAYER

Heart of Jesus, source of consolation, I consecrate myself to you this day. Accept the gift of my heart. I desire to belong to you alone. Take all my thoughts, words, and actions and fill them with your compassion and love. Sacred Heart of Jesus, make me an instrument of your love. Amen

PRAYER OF THANKSGIVING

Loving Heart of Jesus, I give you praise and thanks for granting my special intention. *(Here mention your intention.)* The answer you have given to my prayers fills me with gratitude.

To show my gratefulness, I recommend to your merciful heart the needs of anyone among my family and friends that is in most need of your merciful love. *(Here mention the person you are praying for.)*

Sacred Heart of Jesus, be my peace and consolation. Amen

(Finish by praying the Litany of the Sacred Heart, page 58.)

To the Infant Jesus of Prague

Feast Day: January 2

PRAYER OF PETITION

Lord Jesus, your greatest joy was to live here on earth among us. Bless me this day, and help me to have confidence in your love and compassion. I honor you as the Holy Infant of

Prague and dedicate myself to you. Give me the grace to live my life in union with your commandment of love. May I love you with all my heart, with all my mind, with all my soul. Dedicated to your holy childhood, I ask you to teach me to be gentle and humble. May I bring your message of love and joy to all I meet this day. Infant Jesus of Prague, I present to you my most earnest request. *(Here mention your request.)* Lord Jesus, hear my prayer and bless me. Infant Jesus of Prague, be my comfort!

SCRIPTURE READING
MATTHEW 2:11A

On entering the house, they saw the child with Mary his mother; and they knelt down and paid him homage.

SILENT REFLECTION

REFLECTION PRAYER

Infant Jesus of Prague, many are the wonders you have worked for your people. You made a promise to your servant, Carmelite Father Cyril of the Mother of God: "The more you honor Me, the more I will bless you." Hear my prayer and grant that your promise may be fulfilled in my regard. Thank you for all the blessings you continue to bestow upon us. Glory and praise to you, Lord Jesus Christ!

PRAYER OF THANKSGIVING

Infant Jesus of Prague, I give you praise and thanks for all the ways you have shown your loving kindness towards me. I give you special thanks for _____. *(Here mention your thanksgiving.)* I promise to show my gratitude for the favors received by many acts of service and kindness to my sisters and brothers. I do this in your name. Praise to you Lord Jesus Christ, now and forever! Amen

In Honor of the Holy Angels

Feast Day: October 2

All you Angels of God, who stand before the throne of the Lamb, give the Lord glory and praise forever.

Blessed Spirits, our guardians and intercessors, you are given to us by the loving providence of God as our companions on the journey of life. We call upon you to assist us in a special way this day. Many are the difficulties and anxieties that sometimes surround us. We turn to you, Angels of God, and ask you to help us in our present need. *(Here make your petition.)*

SCRIPTURE READING
EXODUS 23:20-21A

I am going to send an angel in front of you, to guard you on the way and to bring you to the place that I have prepared. Be attentive to him and listen to his voice.

PRAYER

God has given angels the command to watch over us and protect us in our daily lives. The angel of the Lord is over us to rescue us from all dangers. Blessed be God in the angels and in the saints, now and forever. Amen

SCRIPTURE READING
REVELATION 8:3-4

Another angel with a golden censer came and stood at the altar; he was given a great quantity of incense to offer with the prayers of all the saints on the golden altar that is before the throne. And the smoke of the incense, with the prayers of the saints, rose before God from the hand of the angel.

In Honor of Saint Raphael the Archangel

Glorious Archangel Raphael, healer sent from God, you are one of the seven spirits who stand before the throne of God. Intercede for us in our most urgent need. Just as you helped the young Tobias, you will assist us by your protection and prayers. Great Archangel Raphael, enlighten, defend, and protect me this day. Amen

In Honor of Saint Gabriel the Archangel

Glorious Archangel Gabriel, power of God, you were sent to announce to the Virgin Mary that she was to be the Mother of Christ. Holy ambassador of the Most High, intercede for us in our most urgent need. Great Archangel Gabriel, be our guide and protector in the journey of life. Lead us closer to Jesus and Mary. Amen

In Honor of Saint Michael the Archangel

Glorious Archangel Michael, one who is like God, you are the defender of the Church, protector of the dying, and destroyer of evil spirits. Come to our aid and help us in our present need. Glorious prince of the heavenly spirits, surround us in the light of your powerful protection. Enlighten our minds and inflame our hearts so we may be true witnesses of Jesus Christ, our Lord and Savior. Amen

In Honor of Our Mother of Perpetual Help

Feast Day: June 27

Mother of Perpetual Help, you have been blessed and favored by God. You became not only the Mother of the Redeemer but the Mother of the Redeemed as well. We come to you today as your loving children. Watch over us and take care of us. As you held the child

Jesus in your loving arms, so take us in your arms. Be a mother ready at every moment to help us, for God who is mighty has done great things for you, and God's mercy is from age to age on those who love God. Our greatest fear is that, in time of temptation, we may fail to call out to you and become lost children. Intercede for us, dear Mother, in obtaining pardon for our sins, love for Jesus, final perseverance, and the grace always to call upon you, Mother of Perpetual Help.

Mother of Perpetual Help, pray for us.

PROCLAMATION OF PRAISE
IN HONOR OF MARY

Glorious and wonderful things are said about you, our Virgin Mary. You are the glory and joy of the Christian people. You are the defender of the poor and rejected. You are the safe refuge of the persecuted and a mother ever ready to help us. Surround us with the radiance of your loving protection, and keep us safe from all that would harm us, glorious and powerful Mother of the Redeemer.

SCRIPTURE READING
JUDITH 13:20, CCB

May God ensure your everlasting glory, and may he reward and bless you for you have risked your life when your race was humiliated. You chose instead to do the best before God in order to prevent our downfall.

SILENT REFLECTION

PETITIONS

(Remember your intentions and those of others at this time.)

PRAYER

Mother of Perpetual Help, we your children come before you. You know the desire of your son who wishes to share with us the fullness of redemption. We ask you to assist us with your prayers. Mother of Christ, during the passion and death of your son, he gave you to us as a mother. You ask us to call you Mother of Perpetual Help. In confidence we present our needs to you and trust in your motherly care for us. Gather us together under your protection, and lead us one day to share with you and all the angels and saints the joys of heaven. Amen

LITANY

Holy Mary,   **R. Pray for us.**
Mother of Jesus,
Tabernacle of the Holy Spirit,
Mother of the Poor,
Health of the Sick,
Consoler of the Suffering,
Mother of Perpetual Help,

Let us pray.

All powerful and merciful Lord, you give us the picture of the Mother of your Son to venerate under the title of Our Mother of Perpetual Help. Graciously grant that in all the difficulties of our lives we may be assisted by the continuous protection of the Virgin Mary and obtain the reward of eternal redemption. You who live and reign forever and ever. Amen

In Honor of Our Lady of Guadalupe

A great sign appeared in heaven: a woman, clothed with the sun, with the moon under her feet and a crown of twelve stars on her head.

Revelation 12:1, CCB

Glorious Mother of the Redeemer, Compassionate Lady of Guadalupe! You are the glory of your people, the chosen vessel of God. In your loving concern for your people, you appeared to Juan Diego and revealed yourself as the mother of mercy and love. We come to you with our petitions. *(Here make your peti-*

tions for the novena.) Hear our prayers, and show yourself a mother ever ready to assist us in our needs.

Who is this coming like the dawn, fair as the moon, bright as the sun? It is you, Holy Mother of our Savior. You are the mystical rose, the mother of the afflicted, the defender of the oppressed. Obtain for us a strong faith and ardent charity. Form us into a people eager to proclaim Jesus as our Lord. Hear us, beautiful Lady of Tepeyac, our Lady of Guadalupe.

Hail Mary....
V. Our Lady of Guadalupe,
R. pray for us who have recourse to you.

Most glorious Virgin Mary, Mother of God, look with kindness upon us, your children. Many are the difficulties that surround us in our Christian journey. In times of danger, be at our side with your protection. Help us to live our lives, faithful to the gospel of Jesus. Following your example, may we listen to the

Word of God and surrender our lives to the action of the Holy Spirit. Pray for us, loving Mother of our Redeemer! Amen

In Honor of Our Sorrowful Mother

Feast Day: September 15

Near the cross of Jesus stood his mother, his mother's sister Mary, who was the wife of Cleophas, and Mary of Magdala. When Jesus saw the Mother, and the disciple, he said to the Mother, "Woman, this is your son." Then he said to the disciple, "There is your mother." And from that moment the disciple took her to his own home.

John 19:25-27, CCB

Mother of Sorrows, your heart was pierced by a sword of sorrow as you gazed upon the suffering and death of your beloved Jesus. I come before you with confidence that you will help me, for in your wounded, sorrowing heart I find a place of comfort and peace. I beg you, Mother of the Savior, to listen to my request. *(Pause here and make your request.)* For to whom shall I have recourse in my needs, if not to you, Mother of compassion and love? As you gazed upon your dying Jesus, you united your *fiat* to his cry of surrender: "Father, into your hands I surrender my spirit." I unite myself to you, Mother of mercy, and beg you to unite my sufferings with yours and offer them to Jesus. For you are our life, our sweetness, and our hope. Amen

The First Sorrow:
The Prophecy of Simeon

Simeon blessed them and said to Mary, his mother, "See him; he will be for the rise or fall of the multitudes of Israel. He shall stand as a sign of contradiction, while a sword will pierce your own soul. Then the secret thoughts of many may be brought to light."

Luke 2:34-35, CCB

Hail Mary.…
V. Virgin Most Sorrowful,
R. pray for us.

The Second Sorrow:
The Flight into Egypt

After the wise men had left, an angel of the Lord appeared in a dream to Joseph and said, "Get up, take the child and his mother and flee to Egypt, and stay there

until I tell you. Herod will soon be look-
ing for the child in order to kill him."

Joseph got up, took the child and his
mother, and left that night for Egypt,
where he stayed until the death of Herod.

Matthew 2:13-15, CCB

Hail Mary....
V. Virgin Most Sorrowful,
R. pray for us.

The Third Sorrow:
The Loss of Jesus in the Temple

After the festival was over, they returned,
but the boy Jesus remained in Jerusalem
and his parents did not know it. On the
first day of the journey they thought he
was in the company and looked for him
among their relatives and friends. As they
did not find him, they went back to
Jerusalem searching for him.

Luke 2:43-45, CCB

Hail Mary.…

V. Virgin Most Sorrowful,

R. pray for us.

The Fourth Sorrow:
Mary Meets Jesus
on the Way to Calvary

A large crowd of people followed him; among them were women beating their breast and wailing for him, but Jesus turned to them and said, "Women of Jerusalem, do not weep for me, weep rather for yourselves and for your children."

Luke 23:27-28, CCB

Hail Mary.…

V. Virgin Most Sorrowful,

R. pray for us.

The Fifth Sorrow:
Jesus Dies on the Cross

When Jesus saw the Mother, and the disciple, he said to the Mother, "Woman, this is your son." Then he said to the disciple, "There is your mother."

John 19:26-27, CCB

Hail Mary....
V. Virgin Most Sorrowful,
R. pray for us.

The Sixth Sorrow:
Mary Receives the Dead Body
of Jesus in Her Arms

Joseph of Arimathea boldly went to Pilate and asked for the body of Jesus....Joseph took it down and wrapped it in the linen sheet he had bought.

Mark 15:43,46a, CCB

Hail Mary.…

V. Virgin Most Sorrowful,

R. pray for us.

The Seventh Sorrow:
Jesus Is Placed in the Tomb

He [Joseph] laid the body in a tomb which had been cut out of the rock and rolled a stone across the entrance to the tomb.

Mark 15:46b, CCB

Hail Mary.…

V. Virgin Most Sorrowful,

R. pray for us.

Let us pray.

Lord Jesus Christ, the prophecy of Simeon that a sword of sorrow would pierce the heart of your beloved Mother was fulfilled in her as she stood beneath the cross. May we who have commemorated with devotion her seven sorrows be united with her in offering our lives

in loving surrender to your sacred passion.
Amen

(Finish by praying the Litany of the Immaculate Heart of Mary, page 62.)

In Honor
of Saint Joseph

Feast Days: March 19 and May 1

This is how Jesus Christ was born. Mary his mother had been given to Joseph in marriage but before they lived together, she was found to be pregnant through the Holy Spirit. Then Joseph, her husband, made plans to divorce her in all secrecy. He was an upright man, and in no way did he want to discredit her. While he was pondering over this, an angel of the Lord appeared to him in a dream and said, "Joseph, descendant of David, do not be afraid to take Mary as your wife. She has conceived by the Holy Spirit, and will bear a son, whom you are to call 'Jesus' for he will save his people from their sins."

Matthew 1:18-21, CCB

PRAYER

Glorious Saint Joseph, spouse of Mary and foster father of Jesus our Savior, hear our plea for help and protection. Help us to listen to the voice of God speaking in our lives. Guide us to follow the will of God when it is manifested in our lives. You protected Jesus and Mary and provided for their earthly needs. Look upon the petitions we present to you this day. Saint Joseph, most loving of fathers, hear and grant our requests. *(Here make your requests.)*

The Memorare of Saint Joseph

Remember, most pure spouse of the Blessed Virgin Mary, my protector Saint Joseph, that no one has ever had recourse to your protection or implored your assistance without obtaining relief. Confiding in your goodness, I come to you and humbly ask you to hear my petitions, gentle foster father of the Redeemer. In your love, hear and answer me. Amen

PRAYER OF THANKSGIVING

Glorious Saint Joseph, I honor you, and I thank you for having assisted me in my time of need. To show my gratitude, I will extend charity toward my neighbor, especially the person you choose to send to me. I pray for all those who are most in need of your fatherly help. Saint Joseph, pray for us!

How to Make a Novena in Honor of a Special Saint or Patron

You can begin your time of prayer with the first part of this service. Then, if this booklet contains a prayer to your patron, go to the Novena Prayers section (pages 44-57) and pray the prayer to your patron.

If your special saint is not in this booklet, you can still make a novena by using the following format. It would be good to look up the life of your saint in a book of saints so as to become familiar with the life and virtues of your favorite heavenly patron.

Conclude with the prayer to a special saint or patron.

In Honor of a Special Saint or Patron

OPENING PRAYER

Blessed be God in the angels and in the saints.

SCRIPTURE READING
REVELATION 7:9-10

After this I looked, and there was a great multitude that no one could count, from every nation, from all tribes and peoples and languages, standing before the throne and before the Lamb, robed in white, with palm branches in their hands. They cried out in a loud voice, saying, "Salvation belongs to our God who is seated on the throne and to the Lamb!"

SILENT REFLECTION

(After pausing in silent reflection, read something from the lives of the saints about your special patron. See if there is something in the

life of the saint that you could imitate in your own life. Then continue with the following prayers.)

PRAYER IN HONOR OF A SPECIAL SAINT OR PATRON

God of love and compassion, you are the source of all that is holy and good. In your great mercy you have singled out _____ for her/his love and faithfulness. I ask that you listen to the prayers of _____ united with my own prayer of petition and grant my most urgent need. *(Here mention your requests.)* May the example of _____ inspire me to walk in the way of love of God and neighbor. May I one day join with _____ in singing your mercies throughout eternity. Grant this through Christ our Lord. Amen

Novena Prayers

Saint Elizabeth Ann Seton

Feast Day: January 4

Loving God, in Saint Elizabeth Ann Seton you have given us an example of faithfulness and love. As wife, mother, and foundress, she shows us how to live our lives in charity and concern for others. Through her intercession, may she obtain for us our request. *(Here mention your intentions.)* Like Saint Elizabeth Ann Seton, may we have an intense love for Jesus present in the holy Eucharist. Following her example, may we seek our consolation in his holy presence. Amen

Saint John Neumann

Feast Day: January 5

Saint John Neumann, you were filled with desire to leave your homeland and preach the Good News of Jesus Christ in the United States. Teach us to live our lives with a great desire to make Jesus known and loved in the lives of all we meet. Like you, may we have compassion on the needy and the weak. We ask the help of your intercession in our present need. *(Here mention your request.)*

Saint John Neumann, pray for us. Amen

Blessed Brother André, C.S.C.

Feast Day: January 6

Blessed Brother André, you were confident in the power of Saint Joseph to come to the help of people who were in desperate need.

Many people came to you asking for your advice and prayerful support in their daily living. Help us to have confidence in the power of Saint Joseph. Join your prayers with ours as we implore God for our most urgent need. *(Here mention your request.)* Blessed Brother André, pray for us and help us to have confidence in Jesus Christ our Lord. Amen

Saint Katharine Drexel

Feast Day: March 3

Saint Katharine Drexel, our compassionate God called you to serve the poor and oppressed of our country. Through your intercession, help us to respond to the gospel of Jesus by living lives of generosity and love. Hear and answer the requests we now make. *(Here mention your request.)*

Saint Katharine Drexel, help us, like you, to turn to Jesus in the Blessed Sacrament and to trust in the mercy of his Sacred Heart. Amen

Saint Peregrine

Feast Day: May 4

Patron of those who suffer from cancer

Saint Peregrine, you have given us an outstanding example of faith and patience. Through the help of your prayers, bring the healing light of Jesus Christ upon my cancer.

Good Saint Peregrine, pray for me and for the treatment and medicine that I must use. Be with me in all that lies ahead. Help me to have faith and confidence in your prayers for me. Intercede for me and all those who suffer the disease of cancer.

Saint Rita

Feast Day: May 22

Patron of impossible cases

Saint Rita, so humble, pure, and patient, the faithfulness of your love won favor with Jesus Christ. Your pleadings with the Lord are very powerful. Obtain for us from the crucified Savior our request. *(Here mention your request.)* Be gracious toward us for the greater glory of God, and we promise to honor you and to sing your praises forever. Amen

Saint Rita, pray for us!

Saint Anthony of Padua

Feast Day: June 13

Patron of the poor and needy

Saint Anthony, you are called "the great miracle worker." I am in great need of your help. Come to my aid and obtain for me the request I present to you. *(Here make your request.)* Through you, God worked many wonders for people. Miracles happened at your word. I am filled with confidence that you will help and console me in my necessity. Gentle and loving Saint Anthony, may I be the object of your compassionate love. You were filled with ardent love for Jesus. Present my requests to the heart of Jesus and help me to give God thanks and praise. Saint Anthony, wonder-worker, intercede for me. Amen

Blessed Kateri Tekakwitha

Feast Day: July 14

Blessed Kateri, you are a shining example of Christian love among the Native American people. You responded to your baptismal call to follow closely in the footsteps of Jesus Christ. May we imitate you in living our lives with deep affection for Jesus. Help us to accept the difficulties of life with sincerity and peace. Help us in our present need. *(Here mention your request.)* Lily of the Mohawk, teach us how to live the great commandment of love. Following your example, may we fill the world with deeds of compassion and love. Amen

Saint Anne, Mother of the Virgin Mary

Feast Day: July 26

Saint Anne, mother of the Virgin Mary and grandmother of Jesus our Savior, come to our aid! Many are the people who call upon you for help. Listen now to our prayers, help us in our most urgent need. *(Here mention your request.)* Teach us, good Saint Anne, to keep our life centered on God. When temptation and evil come near us, surround us with your powerful protection. In union with you, we join in giving praise and thanks to God our Father for all the blessings given us. Remember all who call upon you for help. Obtain for us a greater love of Jesus Christ and the grace to live the gospel in our daily lives. Amen

Good Saint Anne, pray for us!

Saint Thérèse of Lisieux

Feast Day: October 1

Saint Thérèse, the church honors you as the saint of the "Little Way." Teach me how to transform the ordinary tasks of my day into acts of love for Jesus. I come to you and ask your help. *(Here mention your request.)* You surrendered yourself in loving trust to Jesus. Teach me how to live a life of trust in the mercy of God. You said that you desired to spend your heaven in doing good on earth. Please help me by joining your prayers to mine. Saint Thérèse of the Child Jesus and of the Holy Face, pray for me.

Blessed
Francis Xavier Seelos

Feast Day: October 5

Bountiful God, in Blessed Francis Xavier Seelos you have given your people a model for those who labor joyfully in your earthly kingdom. May his smile dwell on those who find life burdensome. In him, our eyes continually behold the gentleness of Jesus Christ, our Redeemer. Divine Physician, you infused Father Seelos with the gift of your healing. By the help of his prayers, sustain in me the grace to know your will and the strength to overcome my afflictions.

Blessed Francis Xavier Seelos, pray for us! Amen

Saint Jude

Feast Day: October 28

Patron of hopeless cases

Most holy apostle, Saint Jude, faithful servant and friend of Jesus, the Church honors and invokes you universally as the patron of hopeless cases. Pray for me, I am so helpless and alone. Make use, I implore you, of that particular privilege given to you to bring visible and speedy help where help is almost despaired of. Come to my assistance in this great need, that I may receive the consolation and help of heaven in all my necessities, tribulations, and sufferings, particularly *(here make your request),* and that I may praise God with you and all the elect forever. I promise, Blessed Saint Jude, to be ever mindful of this great favor, to always honor you as my special and powerful patron, and to gratefully encourage devotion to you. Amen

Saint Frances Xavier Cabrini

Feast Day: November 13

Saint Frances Xavier Cabrini, you were called "mother" by all who knew you in your lifetime. Show toward us your motherly concern in our special need. We rejoice that you consecrated your life to work among the immigrant people of our nation. In the face of endless cares and anxieties, you trusted in the Sacred Heart of Jesus for your strength. Hear us as we call upon you to help us in our present need. *(Here mention your intentions.)* Mother Cabrini, like you, may we live our lives in service to others for the love of Jesus. Amen

Saint Rose Philippine Duchesne

Feast Day: November 18

**Novena of Confidence in the
Sacred Heart of Jesus**

Lord Jesus, through the intercession of Saint Rose Philippine Duchesne, to your Sacred Heart I confide _____ *(this intention).*

Only look. Then do what your Heart inspires. Let your Heart decide. I count on it. I trust in it. I throw myself on its mercy.

Lord Jesus, you will not fail me!

Blessed Miguel Pro, S.J.

Feast Day: November 23

Blessed Miguel, you responded with a generous heart to the call of Christ. You gave your life in witness to the gospel of Jesus. Help us who strive to follow the way of Christ in our daily lives.

Before your death, you told your friend to ask you for favors when you were in heaven. I beg you to intercede for me and in union with Our Lady and all the angels and saints to ask our Lord to grant my petition, provided that it be God's will. *(Here mention your request.)*

Blessed Miguel, defender of workers, courageous priest, forgiver of persecutors, holy martyr of Christ, pray for us!

Saint Lucy

Feast Day: December 13
Patron of diseases of the eye

Lord Jesus Christ, you are the light of the world! Open our eyes to see your presence in the world. May we always walk in the path of your gospel light. Through the intercession of your servant and martyr, Saint Lucy, heal the disease of our eyes, and give us perfect vision that we may serve your greater honor and glory. Saint Lucy, virgin and martyr, hear our prayers and petitions. Amen

Litanies

Litany of the Sacred Heart of Jesus

*(Repeat the response **(R.)** after each invocation.)*

Lord, have mercy.
Christ, have mercy.
Lord, have mercy.

Christ, hear us.
Christ, graciously hear us.

God, the Father
   of Heaven,   **R. have mercy on us.**
God, the Son, Redeemer of the world,
God, the Holy Spirit,
Holy Trinity, one God,

Heart of Jesus, Son of the
    Eternal Father,   **R. have mercy on us.**
Heart of Jesus,
    formed by the Holy Spirit in the womb of
    the Virgin Mother,
Heart of Jesus, substantially united
    to the Word of God,
Heart of Jesus, of infinite majesty,
Heart of Jesus, sacred temple of God,
Heart of Jesus, tabernacle of the
    Most High,
Heart of Jesus, house of God and
    gate of heaven,
Heart of Jesus, burning furnace of charity,
Heart of Jesus, abode of justice and love,
Heart of Jesus, full of goodness and love,
Heart of Jesus, abyss of all virtues,
Heart of Jesus, most worthy of all praise,
Heart of Jesus, King and center of all hearts,
Heart of Jesus, in whom are all the treasures
    of wisdom and knowledge,
Heart of Jesus, in whom dwells the fullness
    of divinity,

Heart of Jesus, in whom the Father was
    well pleased,   **R. have mercy on us.**
Heart of Jesus, of whose fullness we
    have all received,
Heart of Jesus, desire of the
    everlasting hills,
Heart of Jesus, patient and most merciful,
Heart of Jesus, enriching all who
    invoke your name,
Heart of Jesus, fountain of life and holiness,
Heart of Jesus, propitiation for our sins,
Heart of Jesus, loaded down
    with opprobrium,
Heart of Jesus, bruised for our offenses,
Heart of Jesus, obedient unto death,
Heart of Jesus, pierced with a lance,
Heart of Jesus, source of all consolation,
Heart of Jesus, our life and resurrection,
Heart of Jesus, our peace
    and reconciliation,
Heart of Jesus, victim of sin,
Heart of Jesus, salvation of those
    who trust in you,

Heart of Jesus, hope of those
who die in you,   **R. have mercy on us.**
Heart of Jesus, delight of all the saints,

Lamb of God, who takes away the sins of
the world, have mercy on us.
Lamb of God, who takes away the sins
of the world, graciously hear us, O Lord.

Jesus, meek and humble of heart, make our
hearts like yours.

Let us pray.

O almighty and eternal God, look upon the
Heart of your dearly beloved Son and upon
the praise and sacrifice he offers you on
behalf of sinners. Grant pardon to those who
seek your mercy, in the name of the same Jesus
Christ, your Son, who lives and reigns with
you forever. Amen

Litany of the Immaculate Heart of Mary

*(Repeat the response (**R.)** after each invocation. This litany is for private use only.)*

Lord, have mercy on us.
Christ, have mercy on us.
Lord, have mercy on us.

Christ, hear us.
Christ, graciously hear us.

God, the Father
   of heaven,   **R. have mercy on us.**
God, the Son, Redeemer of the world,
God, the Holy Spirit,
Holy Trinity, one God,

Heart of Mary,   **R. pray for us.**
Heart of Mary, like unto the heart of God,
Heart of Mary, united to the heart of Jesus,
Heart of Mary, instrument of the Holy Spirit,

Heart of Mary, sanctuary
   of the Divine Trinity,   **R. pray for us.**
Heart of Mary, full of grace,
Heart of Mary, blessed among all hearts,
Heart of Mary, throne of glory,
Heart of Mary, most humble,
Heart of Mary, holocaust of divine love,
Heart of Mary, fastened to the cross
   with Jesus crucified,
Heart of Mary, comfort of the afflicted,
Heart of Mary, refuge of sinners,
Heart of Mary, hope of the agonizing,
Heart of Mary, seat of mercy,

Lamb of God, you take away the sins of the
   world, spare us, O Lord.
Lamb of God, you take away the sins of the
   world, have mercy on us.

Immaculate Heart of Mary, pray for us who
   have recourse to you.
Loving Heart of Mary, be our hope and
   consolation.

Let us pray.

O most merciful God, for the salvation of sinners and refuge of the miserable, you were pleased that the pure heart of Mary should be most like in love and pity to the divine heart of your Son, Jesus Christ. Grant that through the sweet and loving heart of Mary, our own hearts may, by her merits and intercession, become like the heart of Jesus. We ask this through Christ our Lord. Amen